NONE OF THIS IS BY ACCIDENT

My Testimony of Wholeness & Healing

TANYA R. BOUDREAUX

Copyright © 2025 Tanya R. Boudreaux.

All rights reserved. No part of this book may be reproduced, stored, or transmitted by any means—whether auditory, graphic, mechanical, or electronic—without written permission of both publisher and author, except in the case of brief excerpts used in critical articles and reviews. Unauthorized reproduction of any part of this work is illegal and is punishable by law.

CONTENTS

Preface — v

Part 1: Embracing the Journey — 1
Understanding the Purpose Behind Our Pain

- Starting the Healing Process: How do I begin to heal? — 3
- The Awakening: Finding Purpose in My Pain — 9
- Stronger Than You Think: You're Going to Be Okay! — 12
- Navigating Fear as an Empath — 14
- Lessons from My Son — 23
- Deciding Not to Feel — 26
- Strength in Solitude: The Isolation — 29
- The Shift: New, Necessary Habits — 31

Part 2: Redefining What It Means to Get Better — 39
From Surviving to Thriving

- How Did I Arrive Here? – Detailing the Process — 41
- It's Okay…to Feel: Accepting My Emotions — 43
- This Day is Tough! — 48

- ➢ The LAST Violation — 50
- ➢ Now Is the Time — 52
- ➢ What If the Pain Comes Back? — 58

Part 3: Recognizing the Transformation — 63
How to Move Forward in Love

- ➢ Learning to Wait Gracefully — 67
- ➢ Letting It All Go — 69
- ➢ Discovering Love Again — 72
- ➢ L – O – V – E: Let's Talk About It — 73
- ➢ Open Letter To My Husband — 75
- ➢ A Mother's Love — 76
- ➢ Takeaways from this section — 78

Something I want you to remember — 79

About the Author — 81

PREFACE

As I laid in bed, I thought about all the amazing men I have met; God allowed me to witness several couples that have all been happily married. For a while, I was beginning to lose hope that there were still good, decent men out here. In the last couple of months, God has allowed me to personally witness how God-fearing men love, respect, support, and protect their wives. There was a certain gentleness about them; they observed their wives, listened to them, responded to even the smallest gestures their wives made, and they were attentive. They protected them, shielded them, and at times catered to them. As I laid in bed, I thought to myself, *God, I really want this; I'm excited to see and meet my husband.*

The very next second, I thought, *You know God, I see these women, and some aren't the best wives to their husbands, while some are, and they have all their needs met and oftentimes catered to.* So, my question is, why did I have to go through the trauma and pain from my marriage and all of the relationships thereafter? Why didn't I get the prized husband that some of these women got? I know my time is coming, and my husband is on his way; I know this because I pray for him daily. But I would be lying to myself if I didn't admit that I do get discouraged at times, so the thought does cross my mind more often than I would like to admit as to why I experienced so much pain. God knows that I crave to be held, I desire human touch, and I deserve the love of a man who can see and love me in the way that God meant a man to love a woman, but it seems as if my circumstances and some of my choices led me down a path of heartache and pain, and for the love of me, I just can't seem to figure out why.

Lord, I've been single for quite some time now. I've also gone through a rather long healing journey, and I believe that I am ready for the union with my husband. While I was speaking to God, it dawned on me how much my relationship with him has grown and how much I truly trusted God throughout my healing journey; otherwise, I wouldn't have been able to be so transparent and honest in my conversation with him. My level of comfort with God felt amazing; I could speak to God about my innermost thoughts and fears, knowing that I was encapsulated by his love.

This is what I know and can recall from my healing journey. First, I was never trying to question God or cast doubt on my prayers; I was simply talking to him and trying to find clarity on the trauma and pain I have experienced. Second, I can personally attest to the fact that God has yet to let me down on anything in life, so although this journey was tough, I knew I would be okay. Third, at the time I was writing this, I was truly focused on my future husband, and because of my focus on God and his track record of answering prayers, I know God will reveal my husband when we are both ready. My healing journey required me to deal with a lot of hurt and trauma from my past, so as I write this book, it will allow you to capture bits and pieces of my healing journey, but more importantly, I hope to provide you with a tried and tested process to a successful healing journey. As far as my future husband, I look forward to our union.

My healing journey has transferred me into the happy, peaceful, loving, successful, beautiful, amazing, spiritual, loyal, and phenomenal woman I am today. A few months ago, I would have never been able to utter those words and believe them. I wasn't angry, nor was I bitter; I was just uncomfortable in my skin and very doubtful of the possibility of true love. When I thought about a possible relationship and the opportunity presented itself, I would jump at the chance to commit. I would jump at the chance without setting up the right type of boundaries and standards for being in a healthy relationship, especially if I liked the guy and his company. When I did this, I often let my guard down too fast and exposed my emotional vulnerabilities a little too quickly when I should have slowed some things down. Now, time has passed, and healing has occurred; the result is that I am extremely comfortable in my skin and very confident that my next relationship and marriage will be absolutely amazing.

Now, earlier, I posed a question that wasn't rhetorical, and I would like to answer it: why did I have to go through such turmoil, trials, and tribulation? As I was talking to God, the answer came to me: it was for this book. You see, God has allowed me to experience this trauma to be able to relate with you, the one who's reading this book. I have experienced enough emotional pain and heartache that I can probably relate to whatever tragedy you have possibly experienced. He allowed me to go through it because my purpose was great, because I have a burning desire in me to keep going, which allowed me to overcome every adversity I have faced thus far. There is something in me that gives me the strength and the perseverance to keep going and not give up. Because I am strong, I am powerful, I am beautiful, I am royalty, I have my Father's backing – the pain I experienced brought me directly to God's feet, which is directly tied to my purpose.

I am here to say I have been there; I have felt your pain, your hurt, your trauma, your doubt, your fear, your discomfort, your betrayal, and still, I rise. I came through the flames; I crawled out of the cold, wet, dark spaces in my mind. I cried all the tears. I've felt the sting and body aches caused by the violent act of rape, the blow of a fist that belonged to a man that was supposed to love me and only touch me in gentleness. I've heard the gun "click" as it was pointed at my head. I've gasped for air after being choked, and I've swallowed blood from a busted lip. I've felt that big lump in my throat after I've given all I could towards a relationship and then was told, I don't want to be with you anymore, or the infamous words, "Well, I've met someone else." Or how about, "Oh, I forgot to tell you that I had a wife, but we are separated." WARNING: for the ones that say they're separated and tell you how awful their partner is, be careful; I tried it, and it ended with, "I just want you to know that I'm no longer getting divorced; we are getting back together; it's cheaper to keep her. I really want to be with you; I don't love her, but I'm staying for the kids."

I've had a man pursue and convince me that I was what he wanted, just to say he didn't want me anymore. *Sir, you approached me. I was minding my business, and you interrupted me and my peace; why didn't you just leave me alone from the jump?* What about the ones that say, "Oh yeah, I know her. I mean, we may have kicked it, and I spent time with her; but I didn't sleep with her," all while supposedly being in a committed relationship. Or "Yeah, I slept with her, but come on. It was a mistake; it didn't mean anything. Are you upset?" My response to all of these should have been, "Sir, there is the door; please vacate the premises. You are no longer welcome here." I've even met the ones who were bold enough to tell me that they are the man for me, trying to convince me to give them a chance, all while playing games in the background.

I left all of them, but the problem was I stayed longer than I should have, or I chose to still speak and entertain them even after the relationship was over without a real reason as to why. I saw the red flags, and I felt that something was off, but I ignored it because I wanted a relationship and wanted to be loved so freaking bad. Now, I just smile to myself, distance myself from those who aren't genuine, and keep it moving. I don't have the time nor the patience to deal with the immaturity and disrespect of a man who doesn't see the love in me and the value I bring, so you, Sir, are not worth my time.

Now, back to you, my dear reader. I'm here to help you heal. What comes after that is up to you, so let's make it positive, peaceful, and productive. Are you ready to begin? If so, turn the page.

NONE OF THIS IS BY ACCIDENT

My Testimony of Wholeness & Healing

"The best math you can learn is how to calculate the future cost of your current decisions."

PART

01

EMBRACING THE JOURNEY

Understanding the Purpose Behind Our Pain

A successful healing journey does not happen without your willingness to deliberately live the life you want to live. I've been through a lot of emotional trauma and a lot of hurt, which made me realize I had some unresolved pain. What I've learned is that as you go through life and its twists and turns, when it comes to overcoming trauma, the victory is based partially on how you deal with those that caused you the pain, but most importantly, how you handle and deal with *you* after the pain – how you handle the choices you made, how you deliberately manage your innermost thoughts, how you overcome your own worst enemy (you). When the dust settles, and you are faced with the residual effects of the pain caused by others, your decisions on how you choose to deal with the trauma are the real challenge in overcoming adversity and obtaining your overall victory.

We can all sit here and tell our stories about what happened to us, and we would all be right to demand an apology from the culprits who caused us pain, but then my response to you would be, and then what? So, they admitted to the wrongdoing; they acknowledged what they did; that is great. What people say is what they want you to believe, but what people do is who they really are. Watch and observe their patterns. What is an apology if the behavior doesn't change? And for those who do admit their fault, I applaud you if the intent is never to commit that act again.

Now, let's redirect our attention back to you. Now, young lady or young man, tell me, what are you going to do? You see, regardless of whether they admit their guilt or not, you are still stuck with the pain that was caused, and the choice is yours on how to handle the pain. Is an apology ammo for you to keep going and pointing the finger at them? Or will it be enough for you to drop it and move on like you should so you can enhance the life you are already living or start a completely new one? I'll tell you:

live your life as if you have already received the apology if that is what will make you feel better; and if you get the apology you desire, it won't even matter because you have already moved on. Or use the anger that you are directing at them and turn it into the fuel that is going to drive you and catapult you forward to your next chapter in life, get back in the gym, change your diet, start your business, buy your car, reinvent yourself, find your joy my love, because you deserve it!

Starting the Healing Process: How do I begin to heal?

Let's go on a journey on how to properly heal. First, decide what you want, and then focus on that goal and remove any obstacle in its way until you get it. In other words, if what is in front of you or what you are focused on is blocking or is not adding value to accomplishing your goal, don't allow it to distract you; go around or go through it. If the obstacle is another person or thing, you must make a conscious decision to block that person out by not allowing them to occupy time and space in your head. Oftentimes, we want to blame others for our pain, and when you are truly a victim of someone else's actions of hate or aggression, then I would say that it is okay to place the appropriate amount of blame on that or those individuals; but, if you are ready to heal, it is now time to look inwardly and teach yourself how to appropriately heal from the trauma.

I was raped, beaten, and emotionally abused by someone in my past; and for a while, I stayed angry, bitter, and scared to love because I hadn't allowed myself to heal and grow – partially because I didn't know how. My trauma started early in my adult life, so by the time I was twenty-five, I was carrying a huge amount of weight with me. I had a lot of baggage that I packed up daily and carried around with me willingly. Instead of dealing with the pain, I carried it around. I distracted myself by attending to my son, my job, school, and life; and I remained on a rinse-and-repeat cycle, ignoring the pain that I was toting around. I was successful because I used my anger and frustration to fuel my drive and made good professional decisions, which allowed me to be successful in my career while my personal life suffered. I always knew I had changed, and I wasn't the same person I was before the trauma occurred. I didn't want to walk around angry all day; I wanted love, peace, passion, safety, and security, but I was haunted by fear, insecurities, pain, nightmares, panic attacks, and PTSD.

My healing journey started the day after one of the times I was raped when I tried to wash the filth off me, and it continued when I covered up the bruises of being beaten. I lied to others and myself about my relationship challenges, and when I sat across the table from my therapist and told her, "Yeah, he chokes me a lot – well, at least once or twice a week – but he does let go right before I stop breathing. I don't think he will kill me." This is what I had convinced myself: he will always let go right before I stopped breathing. So, I worked on strengthening my neck so maybe he won't be able to choke me so hard next time; that was my way of dealing with trauma. I didn't know how else to deal with it at that time and moment in my life; I had limited resources and no outside support because I was away from family and friends. I had to learn how to fend for myself, demanding for a twenty-year-old girl away from family and no real friends close by. I had to figure out how to survive daily.

When the police were called, and they were able to identify his handprints on my neck from him choking me, he wised up and began hitting me on my body. You see, I had gained weight after the birth of my son. My body was a little thicker, and even though the blows hurt when I got punched in the gut, I didn't bruise as easily. Any blow to the face or neck, I marked and swelled up immediately, so he learned to go low and beat my body. I can recall him slapping me, causing me to see stars like in the cartoons. I can recall being dragged like a little rag doll from my living room to the spare bedroom by my neck and/or hair, or shirt – or maybe all three. I don't know what he grabbed to drag me down the hall; I just know that my body was bent in a weird way. I was being pulled so hard and fast that I was on my knees trying to keep up. The angle and the force that I was being dragged by caused a crick in my neck that lasted for several days.

I can recall having a gun put to my head after the A/C was turned all the way down, and I was forced to strip naked, standing there shivering. He laughed afterwards, saying the gun wasn't even loaded, so I was making too much of a big deal about it. Tell me something, if someone unbeknownst to you just walks up to you and puts a gun to your head, how would you know if it is loaded or not – and honestly, why does that matter? The fact that you have a gun to your head invokes fear. What other reason would anyone else do it? I can recall being told, "You might as well stop breathing because you are already dead," while I was gasping for air. All of these happened on different occasions and were often followed by more hits to the body or him raping me. All of those could have led to my death, but none of them did. So now I sit here and smile because he didn't win; I did!

When you experience trauma on a consistent basis, the neurotransmitters in your brain rewire and can cause you to remain in "fight or flight" mode continuously, which is extremely unhealthy and harmful to your body and nervous system. Now, as I write this, I realize that many of you are living that life right now and have said to yourself, "I'm doing it now, and I'm doing just fine," or "Welcome to my world." Some of you are praying right now, hoping that you can hold on for another day, trying to figure out how to escape the situation you are currently in. And I have those of you who say, "What doesn't kill you will only make you stronger." All of those may be true and accurate statements for certain times and unique situations, but I'm here to say that if you continue to remain in that state, it won't end well. We are not designed to live that way. I'm here to say you can make a choice to live better and heal physically, emotionally, mentally, spiritually, and psychologically, but most of all, spiritually. For those of you who have escaped that life but are still haunted by the memories and the nightmares, I'm going to fast forward a few years past my trauma so we can get to the healing process.

My real healing journey began the moment I realized that I was tired of being unhappy, tired of being scared, tired of hiding in the background, and tired of not setting boundaries. I realized that I had transitioned from wanting to heal to healing when I started looking forward to real, true unconditional love, waking up with a smile on my face, traveling, laughing, singing, praying, dancing, and living my best life. Read the book 'The Power of the

Subconscious Mind' by Joseph Murphy. It will change your life. Now, let's chat.

I was in Japan – I forgot to say I am active-duty military, and I have been in the Army now for twenty-six years – walk with me as I take you on my journey. I had just arrived in Japan; I was alone, in quarantine because it was amid COVID-19, so isolation was forced upon me. I have always been a spiritual person and have always had a relationship with God. The closeness of our relationship varied on my healing journey and where I was in the process. I had just lost my grandmother the year prior, and all of a sudden, my relationship with my son took a turn for the worse. My stress level was high because I was working nonstop, but God was working in the background to position me in a place where I could heal appropriately. I realize that now, but at the time, I was heartbroken in a way I don't think words could explain. I began to pick at my hair; I was so stressed that my hair began to break and just fall out in pieces. I was broken in a different way than a typical heartache. I was so sad, lonely, afraid, and unsure of the person who was looking back at me in the mirror, and God knew. He also knew that I had been diligently praying and asking to heal, but he knew that I wouldn't do it with all the distractions around me. So he separated me from everything I knew and isolated me; that's when the real healing journey began.

The Awakening: Finding Purpose in My Pain

In Japan, I had quiet time with God. My heart was empty of feelings, because I made a conscious decision to shut off my feelings. I allowed myself to keep enough emotion in me to function at work and do my job, but I shut down all personal feelings. I thought to myself, *If the one person who is supposed to love me unconditionally chooses to separate himself from me, then I can't bear this. I am unable to process these feelings of pain, guilt, shame, uncertainty, and fear, so I will turn them off.*

And that's when the dreams begin again, or shall I say, the nightmares. You see, my physical trauma of rape and physical abuse occurred a while ago, and I would suffer from horrible nightmares back then; but, I thought I had healed from nightmares until Japan. I would dream of snakes rising at the end of my bed, falling on me, being thrown on me, being forced on me by someone else, being in a snake pit, being bitten by them, or just around me watching me. I would wake up screaming or jumping.

It was 2021 in Japan; I was in my room by myself. It was nighttime, and I was in somewhat of a deep sleep. My dreams were so lucid and vivid that I would wake up gasping at times, my heart would be racing, or my screams in my dreams would cause me to wake. The dream that stands out the most is the one where a man entered my room. I heard footsteps walking down the hall (I lived in barracks while in Japan); he opened my door and entered my room. He had walked down the hallway, walked in front of my bed, then over to the side of my bed, and stood over the top of me, just staring at me. I could hear him breathing; I could feel his breath. He wasn't there to hurt me, but I was scared and terrified because it felt so real. I knew he wasn't there to hurt me, but he stayed there for a while and just watched me, and then he tapped me. I didn't feel threatened, but he wanted me to acknowledge his presence. He didn't say anything. He just stood there and waited. I never looked up.

The next morning, I used the Internet to search lucid dreams and what it meant when you dream of a man standing over you. It read, "Refers to the start of some new journey or life path. You have crossed the line in some situation. You are on the fast track to success. The dream represents your hidden potential and latent talents. Someone is pushing you beyond your limits. It also signifies how you really feel about something. You need to stop pleasing others and start thinking about what is best for you. You are being rewarded and recognized for your generosity and giving nature."

Now, when you search online for things like this, several things pop up, but the link I clicked stated the above, and honestly, that was an accurate assessment of what was going on in my life. I was being pushed beyond what I thought my limits were.

This realization scared me, but I was intrigued and a little confused. I had no idea what was going on or what was about to occur. A few nights later, in another dream state, someone entered my room again. This time, I was on the other side of the bed so he didn't have to walk around. I was on the same side as the door, so he had a direct route to me. This time, it was a different man.

This time, he spoke, and it was a familiar voice that said, "I came here to wake you, but I see that you are still asleep, so I'll wait."

I knew the voice, so I had no reason to be scared; he was my cousin Jarvis – well, more like my brother because we grew up together. I called him the very next morning and told him everything.

He responded and said, "Sounds like an awakening to me."

When I searched what it means when someone wakes you in a dream it read, "It is a good sign because it symbolizes freedom and escape. You will embark on tasks that have been assigned in your life, which will automatically result in positive situations. If in the dream you are awakened, it denotes that success will be yours. New opportunities are opening before you, and you need these to make sure that you get the most from life. If you experience a spiritual awakening in your dream, this implies that you identify new challenges in life."

There was more, but it was all good. I was excited. That was the beginning of my true healing journey. A year and some change later, I'm in Germany, separated and isolated from everyone again, with no family, no friends, just me, a huge empty house, and my job. Let's open the door to how I healed, and maybe this will allow you to heal, too.

Stronger Than You Think: You're Going to Be Okay!

I was in my spare bedroom; it was dark. All the lights were off in the room, and that room got *dark*. I had my back up against the wall. So, I sat there silently, content but somewhat unsure of what was next. I felt this feeling in me; I knew my future was being mapped out. I knew sitting there that it would be something big, something huge. I just couldn't quite see what. I'm speaking about this feeling because it began to grow inside me, meaning I had to make room for it. All that baggage that I spoke about in the beginning had to go; I couldn't continue to carry the weight of my past with me and make room for my future. Something had to give.

Due to my isolation, my prayer life began to take off. It

became a requirement for me to find time to talk to God. Most of the time, I would get on my knees to pray, often sobbing with tears, while other times begging for relief from my pain. Many times, I was just simply thanking God for all my blessings and the ability to access him, but this time I just sat. I sat on the floor in the dark and just waited – not praying for anything, not asking for anything, not saying anything. I sat silently; it was so quiet in that room in the dark while sitting against the wall on the floor. It was weird. Why was I there? I was comfortable, however, slightly uncomfortable in the stillness, the peacefulness, and the quietness of the darkness. This was only one room in the house, and like I said earlier, the darkest room in the house. The house I was in was big and empty – just me – so I could hear every sound, every crack, every peep, everything; but everything was completely silent.

There was a fear that came over me when I sat in complete silence and had to meet and face all my thoughts, revisit all my pain, my memories, things that I thought I had overcome, things that I thought were gone.

"Hello," a little voice in my head whispered to me. "We have some work to do."

At the time, I responded inwardly and said, "No, actually, we don't. You see, I have already dealt with this; I am good!"

The voice replied, "I'll be back," and just like that, things went silent again.

I sat there a little bit longer, and that is when it hit – a hurricane of pain, a tornado of emotions, a whirlwind of hate, fear, bitterness, and confusion. The lump in my throat thickened, the pain grew, and the tears began to fall. I began to sob uncontrollably, knowing that I would be okay. I was safe, and I was in a safe place all by myself, alone in a room on the floor against the wall in the dark. I sat there, and I transitioned from silently crying to wailing and then to sobbing uncontrollably at times, but I was safe, safe in God's arms. He held me without me even knowing he was wiping every tear that fell as I wept. All that emotion was being pulled out of me or forced out by that feeling that was in me that let me know there was so much more out there for me. I knew that there was so much I had yet to experience, and all that pain and all that promise couldn't physically reside in one body, so one had to go. The pain, the hurt, the guilt, the hate, the uncertainty, the fear was leaving. That was **stage 1**.

Navigating Fear as an Empath

If you are not careful, FEAR will consume you. As a child, I was afraid of feathers (don't ask me why because I honestly have no idea). I'm no longer afraid of feathers, but I do remember the time I ran from a busted pillow that was stuffed with feathers (Don't judge me). I have always been afraid of snakes, and as I have gotten older, I am no longer deathly afraid of them; however, I am very cautious around them, and I still don't care for them.

As I journeyed through life, I have become very afraid of pain, particularly emotional pain. I am what you may know of as an empath or, as my girlfriend Carla says, a highly sensitive person. I feel things intensely, both good and bad. Little things, big things, and other people's pain affects me also, especially my loved ones. While in the presence of others, I can often feel what they feel or can take on their emotions at times, often without realizing it. Now, I have adopted methods to prevent this from happening, like asking myself if this is my pain or someone else's; it even happens over the phone at times. If someone calls and speaks with me, they end up feeling better, and I'm left feeling sad, lonely, and depressed, like *What just happened?* Transfer of emotions just like that, so empaths, please be careful. My friends and sometimes people, in general, even complete strangers, often confide in me and feel better after speaking with me. I absorb some of that negative energy without realizing it, so they leave relieved and feeling much better, and now I'm carrying that weight.

As I've matured and realized what was occurring, I now place a mental barrier between me and whomever

I'm speaking with to prevent myself from absorbing all, or any, of their energy. The "plus" to this gift is that I can easily tap into someone's inner emotions and oftentimes help them articulate how they are feeling. This allows me to try to help them resolve their challenges or concerns. Of course, the person must be willing to open up to me for that to occur. If a person is just angry, negative, or bitter, I feel that too; I just block myself from absorbing that bad low vibrational energy.

At times when I am just working and "in my zone", at the end of the day, if I had to interact with a lot of people, I sometimes realize I'm a little more tired than usual. This means I forgot to put my barrier up, blocking all those energy fields that are easily absorbed without my noticing. This means that when I am close to someone, especially in a romantic way, I can easily pick up what they are feeling. Sometimes, empaths don't realize how easily we can tap into others' emotions and often try to relieve them of their hurt and pain or try to be too understanding with them because we want them to know that we are there for them, that we are loyal and trustworthy. Be careful; this can backfire on you.

Most people don't want someone in their head and to know their emotional state at all times. They often want the chance and the opportunity to process their thoughts before you start coming in, trying to help dictate how they feel. Let them ask you first, or allow them to vocalize their thoughts before you project yourself onto them. If you, as an empath, overstep and smother someone with your willingness to be so understanding, you may inadvertently push that person away; you must wait until they invite you in. On the flip side, you also must be careful of those who will take advantage of your good heart and your ability to understand their pain. If the person only has you in their life to manipulate and misuse you, more often than not, you, the empath, will end up hurt because the same effort you are giving them will not be reciprocated. When I found myself in a situation where I was giving more effort than my partner, I often ended up hurt, broken-hearted, and in a pool of tears, trying to figure out how I ended up there.

Hello, news flash – I put myself there. I saw the red flags, I felt the shift in their behavior, but instead of pulling away, I pushed more and became that much more understanding until I placed myself in a pool of pain because there was no reciprocity. Which brings me back to the topic of fear. You see, I gave too much too soon, which left me dreading the pain that came along with the heartache. I realized that my biggest fear was not a physical object; what I feared most was the pain of heartache! So, I avoided it like the plague.

"Why does it hurt so much?" I asked God. "I don't

want to hurt anymore. God, please make it stop. I can't deal with this anymore; I just don't want to. Please, God, please make it stop."

Those were the words I said while sobbing for some type of emotional relief. It felt like my whole body would ache when I experienced heartache. I would experience emotional and physical pain, and my entire body would hurt. If you have ever had the flu or COVID body aches, it was nothing like that. It felt like a weight. I felt heavy, like something had latched on to me and just placed all its weight on me; and it hurt – nope, not depression, weight. I felt it in my chest. My heart physically ached. The lump in my throat would grow to where I couldn't swallow – and when I did, it would burn. My stomach would ache; it would be in knots. I couldn't even eat; food repulsed me and made me nauseous. Nothing I did would make it go away, so I would cry. I didn't even want to cry, but the tears would just fall. The ocean of emotions would just overwhelm me, and I would be forced to just sit with my pain and let these feelings run their course; it was torture. I would repeatedly ask God why it hurt so much, what I did to deserve this, and how I could make it stop. I would beg God, plead with him, "Please, God, I'm begging you, can you just make it stop?"

I feared the pain of heart ache so much that I believe deep down I told myself to avoid love – the thing I desired and deserved the most, I subconsciously sabotaged it to avoid pain. I even tried to rationalize to myself that maybe single life is the best for me. Now hear me well, I like my single life; but I will love my married life. We are not made to be by ourselves forever; it will get better. If you are reading this and you can feel my words and the tears are falling, hang in there. I promise you it will get better.

When I was in the phase of trying to convince myself to remain single, I would tell myself, "I don't have to worry about the pain anymore." Minutes later, sometimes seconds, I would say, "Nah, single life is not for me. I need love. I want love. I deserve love. I am love." Then my tears would dry up, and my question would transition from "Why God?" to "Where is he, Lord? Where is my husband?" I would then go into my spiel to God and explain to him, "You see, God, I need him; I crave his touch. I deserve his love. I want his guidance, and I require his protection. Is he looking for me? Have we met? If so, when is he coming? Do you need my address, Jesus?"

My talks with God always ended with me smiling, and he listened the entire time. Every time I rambled, all the times I complained, every time I tried to explain to him exactly what I needed, he sat and listened. He listened to me for hours, with tears rolling down my face. When I screamed in agony and when I begged for relief, my God, your God, our God was always listening; he was and has always been there. It seemed like at the end of my rants, he would pick me up – because most of the time, I was on my knees, sitting on the floor, or sprawled out over the bed – give me a pep talk, and send me on my way. If it was in the morning before work, he would mend my heart little by little, help me wipe my tears, tell me to smile, and remind me who I was. I am royalty; I am his child, and although this healing journey was painful to me, I was on my way to getting better. Through the trauma, I had lost sight of who I was, and he was now on the journey with me every step of the way to help me regain my strength and find my way back. If it was at night, he would pick me up, tuck me in, and place this barrier of protection over me to help me sleep through the night, allowing my body and my heart to heal from the stressors and pain it was carrying from the day.

What does a broken heart look like? Everyone is different, so what I am about to explain to you is my version of how I would explain my heart. I had been through so much emotional pain because the way I process emotion is all in or nothing, so dealing with heavy emotional baggage and pain not only weighed on me but also caused scar tissue over my heart. When I visualize my heart, I see it as being covered with scar tissue, but not just one layer – I had two and three layers of black, scabby scar tissue on my heart. Imagine a red beating heart; now, imagine a scab after you skin your knee or elbow. That skin is thin, so it bleeds easily and a lot when you first cut yourself. Now, picture the scab that forms to cover that wound. If it is a deep cut, the thicker the scab because of all the layers of skin that were damaged – and the longer it takes to heal. I run occasionally, so I have a few scabs on my knees from not paying attention to the terrain and running on uneven pavement where I slipped, tripped, or fell and skinned my knee.

It hurts, and it takes a while to heal. Now, imagine *just* when it's healing up well. It's not painful to the touch anymore, and it doesn't hurt when you brush against it. You reinjure that same spot on that same knee. The cycle begins again. You bump that spot when walking, and now it bleeds because you disrupted the healing process. The scab came off, and now it's bleeding again. This has happened to my heart so many times that my heart was covered in thick black scabs, some thicker than others, while some areas had fresh scabs – some areas were in the healing process, while others were old and thick. Notice I said scabs, not new skin, not keloids, just scabs. So even though my heart was healing, it was not healing fast or finishing the healing process; it was just scabbed all over. I had one little, tiny spot, maybe the size of a dime, where my heart had not been injured. If you can picture a heart scabbed over, and right up at the top was a tiny dime-sized circle where you can see the vibrant red, fresh, healthy heart unscabbed;

that was my saving grace. It was a reminder of what my heart used to be, and that is what God used to bring me back and my heart back to life again. Let me explain.

It wasn't until much later, after I had that same cry and that same prayer, begging, pleading, and sobbing theatrically to God, that I realized I must do something different. *There has got to be more to me than this. I know I deserve better, so tell me, God, what is it that I need to do? Help me!* I had cried and said that prayer countless times on separate occasions before I asked God what I needed to do. You see, prior to asking that question, I would just cry and beg God to heal my heart, but this time it was different. I was done with the tears; well, at least, I thought I was done. I decided that I was ready to face the journey of healing, so I thought. Little did I know, I was just in a phase of my healing journey, and a heavier weight was about to fall on me unexpectedly. I went through something worse than heartache, well, from my perspective, a tragedy that almost broke me. My son, my heartbeat, and my every reason for living began to distance himself from me and decided to stop communicating with me.

Now, anyone who knows me knows the relationship I had with my son. Here is where, as a mom, I messed up and what I didn't see at the time. You see, I knew that I wasn't having the best outcome with men and relationships for one reason or another, but the one thing I did think and believed was that my son would probably be the only man who would always love me and would never leave me. Then, my worst fear happened. How do you deal with that – the loss of someone who is still alive? The grief and pain that exist with that is unbearable, completely debilitating, and something that I am unable to put in words at this current moment. Here is what I'll say: my son was transitioning from a boy to a man, discovering who he was and becoming a father without a physical representation of a man in his life to teach him. I'll just leave that there. That is another book for another time; hopefully, one I will write with him.

Lessons from My Son

"When you hurt, I hurt, Mommy," is what he said to me in the car when he was about four years old.

I was in Maryland at the time. I was driving somewhere; my mother was in the passenger seat, and my son was in the back seat, strapped into his booster seat. My mom and I were having a conversation about something. I don't recall what led me to say to her, "Me-Me," that is what my son calls her, "when you hurt, I hurt." Immediately after I said that, my son from the back seat uttered those same words to me without skipping a beat, "Mommy, when you hurt, I hurt, Mommy."

At that time, I smiled, and my heart melted. It was at that moment I knew he was sent for me. I read somewhere that when a woman gives birth to a son, it's because she was lacking true, unconditional love. That statement didn't really have a significant meaning to me until I heard my son repeat the same words I had said to my mom. What's crazy is we had been talking for hours, and the whole time, he was in the back seat listening, playing, and doing whatever 4-year-old boys do in the back seat sitting in their booster seat. Out of all the things my mother and I had discussed, that was the one thing he repeated back to me, clearly and without hesitation, and then he went back to what he was doing. My heartbeat was strong at that moment, and a huge piece of that scab fell off. I could see a healthier heart shining through. Look at that! I was being healed at times and didn't even know it. It brings a smile to my face at this very moment.

Another time we were in Maryland, I was going through a really tough time struggling to find a place to stay. I didn't have enough money to pay the bills. I had just finalized my divorce. I was a single parent, and I felt like I had the world's weight on my shoulders. I sat on the steps of whatever building I had just walked out of, and I just put my head down, feeling lost, confused, defeated, and unsure of what to do. My son was still young at the time – around three years old – so he stayed close to me as I trained him to, but he was still a little boy eager to play and get into whatever he could in his vicinity. So he was within eyeshot, but just playing next to the bushes not too far from me.

As I sat on the step and hung my head down, I placed my head in my hands, cupping my chin, and just felt heaviness and a whole lot of uncertainty. I felt so heavy that it felt as if the weight of the world was about to consume me, and just like that, Dai-Von, without me knowing, walked over to me. I hadn't even noticed him coming my way, but he was. I felt his little arms around my neck. No words were spoken; he just hugged me. It seemed like for 10-15 minutes that he just hugged me. It probably wasn't that long, but at that moment, I thought to myself, *Oh my God, how did he know? And how could this little person who's a part of me, only one-fourth my size, hug me and bring me such peace and comfort?*

The weight of the world was lifted just like that, and I thought, *He was sent to me. Thank you, God!* When we link up again, my son, you and I will have so much to catch up on; I miss you and love you always. Talk to you soon!

Now, moving on to my breaking point – in reference to all my emotional baggage, hurt, trauma, heartache, bills, life, etc. – I was lost, confused, hurt, angry, and my heart was in pieces. It broke when my son chose to discover life in his own way. It caused a crack in my foundation of what I knew it to be at that time. You see, I was always able to put myself back together again after romantic heartache or any other type of setback, but when your heart shatters, you are in complete disarray. At times, I cried, moped, wept, screamed, and, of course, begged God to fix it, but nothing was changing. I was breathing, but I was walking around in a shell of a body with no life in me. So, I became angry and bitter for about two whole seconds. I don't stay in that negative emotional space for too long; it's just not who I am. However, what I *did* do was not any better. My default setting or my weakness is the inability to properly address and handle my emotions, which oftentimes debilitate me. I allowed the sadness, loneliness, embarrassment, and shame to consume me. So, because I chose not to appropriately deal with my pain, I carried it with me everywhere I went. This occurred prior to me going to Japan, so I took all of that extra baggage with me.

Deciding Not to Feel

You know the emotions that come from abuse don't just leave when you walk away from the abuse, especially if you don't deal with the emotions head-on. So yes, I was abused physically, mentally, emotionally, psychologically, financially, and worst of all, sexually. Because of all of this, anytime I experienced a significant amount of pain, a veil of darkness would come over me like a dark cloud that would hover and hang over me. At times I could even see it – my demeanor changed, my body slouched, my voice changed – because negative emotions stick and cling to you like black tar. When I allowed my emotions to consume me, I was no longer my true self.

There are many different negative emotions, but the ones that cling to me the most are shame and embarrassment. The abuse had me ashamed that I allowed myself to endure that type of trauma and abuse. I was always embarrassed by the bruises and the marks on my body that I covered up and then pretended like everything was fine. The shame you carry with you when you are in an abusive relationship can consume you if you allow it to. So, when my son stopped responding to me, I was ashamed because I thought only a bad parent would have a child that would stop speaking to them. When you take that mindset and you couple that shame with the fear of my son never speaking to me again, the weight of those two heavy emotions silenced me.

For the first time, I didn't know what to pray for, what to ask God for, who to be angry with, or how to manage any of my emotions, so I sat in silence. Yes, I voiced my challenges to those I trusted, and I spoke to the ones that were close to me; but when those conversations were over, and you are by yourself, alone in a room with no other choice but to sit and face your pain and fear, then what, what do you do? I didn't know, and honestly, no one else knew either, so I sat in silence, lifeless, emotionless, and hopeless. I shut down completely as if I had made a choice to turn off every emotion in my body. You know how you can put an electronic device in sleep mode; only the things that are required to keep it running stay on, and everything else shuts down. I had a switch in my head that you are not supposed to touch, and I turned it off. You see, if you could imagine a house with several rooms, now go into a room in the back of the home, and in the corner of that room, off to the side tucked away and definitely not noticeable, there was a door that led to another room. I had this room in my head, and in that room, I had a closet, and in that closet, I had a vault that only I had the code to, and in that vault was a box, and in that box was a key, and that key unlocked and even smaller door and that smaller door had a room with a switch that read, "DO NOT TOUCH!" and I flipped it. I turned it off, and just like that, all my emotions shut down, all feelings left, no reset, no reboot, just off, or so I thought. You see, it was either to turn off every emotion or deal with a significant amount of emotional pain. The pain at that time was too much for me to bear, so I chose option one: turn them off. I remained functional, just without empathy or happiness – just the basic bare minimum, and I told myself, *Now I am good; I am okay.* Lies.

Strength in Solitude: The Isolation

Spiritual isolation is quiet, but it's a different kind of quiet, almost tranquil. I was perplexed as to how everything around me could be so quiet; however, my thoughts were so diverse and random, which made my head noisy. The inner me was screaming for a release. I had trapped my emotions inside of me, and they were trying to figure out how to get out. I have a powerful mind – we all do – so from time to time, I was able to silence my thoughts and pause for some peace. God was always with me, and even when I chose not to speak to him on a consistent basis, when I did ask for help, he would help me silence my thoughts. Now listen to what I just said. We are all God's children, and we often make the decision not to speak to God for whatever reasons we have in our head –

> *I am too busy.*
> *I am upset.*
> *I am living my best life.*
> *I want to figure it out for myself.*
> *I know he wouldn't approve.*
> *I'm being selfish.*
> *I am undisciplined.*

I can keep going, but you get the gist. Here is when I started to connect the dots. Be careful what you pray for, because God answers prayers.

I would pray to be more in tune with God, to see what he would have me see, to love how he would have me love, and to forgive how he would have me forgive. Now, at the time, I figured I was just being a good Christian, and I truly just wanted to be a good human being and love people as God wanted me to. Let me tie this together: I just said that I chose not to speak to God. Now imagine as a father how you would feel for your child to just decide to stop speaking to you after you have literally done everything for them. What was happening with me and my son, I had repeatedly been doing to God, and he loves us in ways we can't even fathom. God was answering my prayer of what I asked for; he was only allowing me to experience a fraction of what I was consistently doing to him. The pain that we cause our Father sometimes we don't even realize, ohhhhh, but now I see. And I'm sorry, God, for blocking you out. I did not know, nor did I quite understand the pain that I caused you until now.

I would also remind you that I said even though I chose to distance myself from God and not speak to him at times, when I did ask, he was always there listening, waiting for me to come back around. And when I really couldn't handle the burden, he carried me and eased my pain. What a Father to love us unconditionally like that; shame on us.

Now I see God, and I understand better how much a parent can love a child. I'll just say I'm a little more cognizant and careful of what I pray for and what I ask God for. Knowing this allows me to process and understand that we all go through phases in life, and as parents, we must allow our kids to go through their process and allow God to work in their lives the way he worked and works in ours. All we need to do is be there for them when they come back around – again, that is another book for another time.

The Shift: New, Necessary Habits

The shift happens slowly yet abruptly, so how can I go from being quiet, tranquil, and peaceful and the very next minute, I have neurons and synapses firing in my head at a rate I'm not accustomed to. There are great moments during the healing process when your brain, body, and heart wake up, and the amount of energy you feel at once comes out of nowhere. At one point in time, my brain was moving and functioning at such a rapid pace. I was resolving problems and responding to people all day, that I thought to myself, *Did I even eat today? I should eat.* I kept asking myself, *What is this place and how did I get here?* Well, I know how I got here – I prayed for it: I requested this. I just didn't know what exactly it felt like until now.

Let me speak about the shift and bring you back to the

purpose of spiritual isolation. God isolates us for different reasons, but I can attest that I believe I was isolated to heal. God removed me from every distraction in my life and removed people from my life, as well, by placing them on their own journey. In my isolation, my relationship with God strengthened significantly. A few things occurred: I was forced to face every emotion I had buried or had not fully processed, and I was able to communicate with God more easily and more often. During isolation, God gave me his undivided attention; let me restate this: God's undivided attention is always there. I didn't take him up on his offer until he pulled me away, sat me down, and said, "Listen, young lady, we have some things to do. Correction: you have some things to do, and you can't do them unless you heal. You have a purpose that you are only partially fulfilling and a small portion at that."

Isolation allowed me to be able to hear God's voice in a way I hadn't been able to tap into before. I was able to discern things a little better, my knowledge and wisdom increased, my prayer life went into overdrive, and God and I became best friends. He laughed with me, held me when I cried, and allowed me to scream and point the finger at him at times during my most painful moments. I always apologized later, but the point was he allowed me to heal in the way that I needed to, without any judgment or penalty. He listened, and in turn, I began to listen to him. I became more obedient, more in tune with my inner self, and more at peace. I was happy, imagine that. In my isolation, I became energized. I was secluded, but I began to shift the way I thought from focusing on my problems to becoming more solution driven. I began to have a brain full of answers firing at a speed that I couldn't quite comprehend. This was unusual for me; it was different, but I liked it.

There were times when my brain would be moving so fast, and I wouldn't be able to quiet down my thoughts; in those times, I would stop and ask God for guidance. At times, I was unable to quiet my brain long enough to hear his response, so I thought to myself, *God, how do I balance this?* Here is what I discovered – it was up to me how to balance it. Let me explain.

During my isolation, I began to change the way I prayed. Instead of asking God to fix me or do something for me, or show me something, or guide me, I began to ask him, *God, what is it that you would like for me to focus on?* Or I'd ask, *How would you like for me to proceed in this situation?* Now let me say this: at times, I had to wait and sit in silence for a while and at other times, I would get a message rather quickly. It wouldn't be a voice like some say; it would be a thought, a word that would just pop in. For example, one time when I asked God what he would like for me to focus on, I heard "you." Another time I heard "fear," another time I heard "forgiveness," and another time I heard "discipline." The one that scared me the most was strength. I remember praying and asking God that morning, 'God, what would you like for me to focus on,' and before I could say the word "on," the word "strength" popped into my head. I thought, *Well, that was fast.* Almost instantaneously, I began to worry and get nervous. I thought to myself, *What traumatic event will I have to go through now??* Remember, I fear emotional pain.

What I realized from my healing journey was that as I healed, a lot of unresolved pain and emotional trauma from my past resurfaced, and God knew I was about to go through a healing phase where some things were going to resurface. He was just prepping me to remain strong and steadfast; this is a process. Now, please understand that when I would ask God how he would want me to proceed with something, it was always a tough pill for me to swallow. Let me just add that I didn't really like hearing any of the things God was telling me to do because it required going deeper into working on my inner self, and that, I wasn't used to. Nothing about healing is easy or pleasurable, but it is required to move past the pain.

Getting back to how he wanted me to proceed in things, particularly when I would meet someone new, someone I really liked and saw myself being in a relationship with. I learned from past heartache and pain that I should ask God how he wants me to proceed with this man before telling

God how interested in him I was and how I liked him. Me authentically liking a guy didn't often occur, so when it happened, and I became intrigued by a man, I would get very excited. Well, here enters God. So, I'm doing the right thing and saying, "Okay God, guess what happened today," you know, because we're cool like that where we can just chat. I begin telling him about someone, and as I continue my prayer, I get more serious when I'm speaking to God.

I'm in my quiet place where it is just him and I. After I tell him how important this is to me and how much I'm looking forward to this, I pause and ask God how do you want me to proceed? I hear, "Wait," and just like that, I just sit, and I think to myself, *Maybe he didn't quite hear or understand what I was saying.* So I restate some things, you know, quick summary of how long it's been and how I've been healing and the growth that has occurred and how deserving I am of a good solid healthy relationship (with him being the overall decision maker, of course). I was attempting to reinforce how much trust and faith I had in him. I paused again and asked, "How do you want me to proceed?" and I would either hear "Wait," again before I could complete my sentence or sometimes nothing at all. Because let's be honest, he heard me the first time, already knew what I was going to ask, and yet still chose to listen to me ramble, and he had already given me his answer.

Now, when I pray and God answers, I just stop and

move to something else. I've learned a few things about a healthy relationship with God, but most importantly, it is an honor and a privilege to be in God's presence. To have the rapport and relationship where God responds to you because you are spiritually in place to hear his voice; please know that if he answers you, all you need to do afterwards is listen, acknowledge what he says, and then execute. When we take God's guidance and our actions are in line with what he tells us, things change; your prayers are answered almost instantaneously at times. Trust the process and observe the shift.

Earlier, I talked about how, at times, my brain gets so busy dealing with issues, people, and problems throughout the day – both mine and theirs. When my brain is busy, I would ask God to help me control my thoughts; sometimes it would take a while, or it would only be momentarily. As my relationship with God increased, my bond with him grew because I was obedient and began to listen to his guidance on other things. Now, when I ask for help, he instantly quiets my mind so I can rest. I always thank God first for the gift he has given me and trusting me to help others resolve their problems, but sometimes, it does get overbearing for me. I find my balance through my walk and my journey with God. This is **stage 2**: acknowledge the shift in your relationship with God, and you can find and obtain your internal balance.

TAKEAWAYS FROM THIS SECTION

1. Love: Understand what it is and what it isn't. (Read 1st Corinthians 13)
2. Hope: Remember to always have hope it; creates a positive outlook on life
3. Companionship: We are not meant to be alone

"You'll be pushed to your limits because the next chapter of your life will require a new version of you."

PART

02

REDEFINING WHAT IT MEANS TO GET BETTER

From Surviving to Thriving

It always gets better. You never stay in the same place for too long. You push through, and you become the person that you are meant to be; because when you heal, you begin to see, smell, taste, feel, hear, and breathe differently. You are becoming a new person, a better version of your old self. If you stay where you are, you, my darling, will not progress.

"Trust in the Lord with all thine heart; and lean not unto thine own understanding. In all thy ways acknowledge him, he shall direct thy paths." - Proverbs 3:5-6 (KJV). This is my favorite scripture. When you are tired and drained, turn to God; call out to him, meditate, spend some time with him, ask him for help, and watch how he enters your life. Pay attention to how he directs you. Sometimes, his approach is slow and methodical; other times, it's swift and rapid. Either way, when you focus on God and the solution – instead of focusing on you and the problem – before you know it, your burden has been lifted.

Throughout your journey in your healing process, you may get tired, but you won't be drained of all energy. Your spirit will be renewed; your smile will return. Your inner peace is so profound that you can feel your body rejoicing and your soul relaxing. His presence surrounds you, and positive energy consumes you, and that is how you know he is holding you. You will have internal peace once you have obtained this type and this level of healing with God. Know that he will never let you go. You are safe, secure, protected, and can rest now, and nothing will hurt you as you go through your healing journey. During the healing process, allow God to mend your heart; let him heal you. You may have thought you were broken, damaged, or possibly even destroyed, but you are not. You are being rebuilt in a way that no one can tear you down. You are stronger, you are wiser, you are smarter, and you are at peace with who you are – in other words, you are better!

How Did I Arrive Here? – Detailing the Process

It was a process to get here, in the peaceful, happy space that I am in. You may be thinking to yourself, *It seems as if you are in a good place, and all these words sound great, but how did you get there?* My response to you is, through much prayer and consistent gratitude.

When I pray, this is one of my typical prayers. "Thank you! Thank you, God, for waking me up this morning. Thank you for the roof over my head and the clothes on my back. Thank you for your love, your mercy, and your grace. Thank you for my taste, my touch, my smell, my sight, my hearing, my physical and mental health. Thank you for your love, mercy, and grace (yes, I say that twice). Thank you for being with me every second, every minute, every hour, every day, every week, every month, and every year. Please don't ever leave. Thank you for allowing me to talk to you anytime, any minute, any day without hurt, harm, or danger. Thank you for all that you have done, all that you are doing and all that you will do for me. Thank you for going before me, walking with me, and going after me at times to clean up my mess or to water the seed that you have allowed me to plant. Thank you for being a great Father and friend and for always listening and never leaving me.

Thank you for making me the exact way you did; thank you for helping me to know my worth and my value. Help me to see myself as you see me, to love how you love, to forgive how you forgive, and thank you for my peace that surpasses my understanding. Thank you for giving me the knowledge and the wisdom of knowing what to say, when to say it, or whether to say it at all. Thank you for allowing me to know what to do, when to do it, or if to do it at all. When I speak, allow me to speak from a place of necessity, a place of genuineness, and a place of truth and love. I am happy that I am here. Thank you for loving me, for making me, for giving me the opportunity to fulfill your purpose, to face my fears, and to overcome all obstacles and adversity that tried to prevent me from accomplishing your goal and fulfilling your purpose. I love you, and I thank you for loving me the way that you do. I am truly grateful to be loved and guided by you. Please don't ever leave. I can smile knowing you are always there."

That is one of my typical prayers in the morning before I go to work. Of course, it changes as my challenges arise. During this time, I was battling with being alone, and I kept thanking God for being there with me and asking him to never leave because I was struggling at the time. Now, if you look at the prayer, I thank God for as many things as I can as often as I can because once you do all that, it makes you forget about anything negative.

Think about it: what if you woke up the next morning and you only had the things you thanked God for the previous day? What would you wake up with? As I prayed daily and built my relationship with God, my healing became a part of my daily routine. It was a habit at this point. I had some great days, some good days, and some tough days, but I always woke up the next day fresh and ready to take on the challenges ahead, always with a positive attitude.

It's Okay...to Feel: Accepting My Emotions

It's okay to cry sometimes when it hurts; sometimes can turn into a lot of times, but it is still okay. When you go through the initial brunt of the unveiling of emotions and the tougher days throughout your healing journey, it gets heavy. Here are some recommendations on how to deal with the influx of emotional pain and past trauma that is resurfacing. First, you must acknowledge the pain, recognize it, and don't just allow it to consume you. The pain is real; it's ugly, and it's persistent. Pay attention to it – it is trying to tell you something.

If your pain is being caused by your current relationship, you are not supposed to be there; remove yourself from that type of torture. If you ever had to pray your way out of a situation, please don't return to that place or that situation just to have to pray your way out of it again. Remember who you are and whose you are. You come from royalty, and you are God's child. Remember, he is the king of all kings. You do not have to submit yourself to that type of treatment, run from anyone or anything who wants to deliberately or has deliberately caused you pain. You do not belong in a place like that. There is always a way out. Your God is not a God of fear; remember, he is always with you. Ask him to make a way and clear a path for you, and he will. He will always direct you to the way out. Pay attention to the signs, listen to his voice, and accept his help when he sends it. None of us got to where we are on our own; we all had help and required help at different stages in our lives.

The healing journey occurs in phases; you will think you are okay one minute, and a few minutes, hours, or days later, emotional grief hits you like a ton of bricks. My message to you is, it is okay to feel your pain; allow it to remind you of where you are not supposed to be and to motivate you to where you are going – which is towards spiritual and emotional fulfillment. When you can no longer bear the pain, ask God for help. Remember, God is yoked up with you; he's there to help you carry the burden when it gets too heavy. He's there, he's always been there. He's just simply waiting for you to ask for help.

You may say, "If he knows I need the help, why doesn't he just help me?" That is not how this works. You see, at times when you are in so much pain from your healing journey that you can't speak and ask for help yourself, God will always intervene; however, remember you asked for this healing. So now he waits; he needs you to ask him because he needs you to know that he will show up if you believe in him. He gives us free will, so if you are determined to do it on your own, he will allow it until he deems it fit to enter. If you invite him into your situation early on, often, he will prevent you from getting into these challenging situations that we often find ourselves in.

Now you say, "What if he doesn't come when I call?" From my experience, there are two reasons why God doesn't enter at the time you ask him to. One, he tried to stop you from doing whatever you did, but you didn't take heed to what he had to say. Maybe you tuned him out; maybe you never invited him into your decision-making process. It is possible that you wanted what you wanted at the time and didn't even consider the consequences. Instead of asking God for permission to proceed, you told him what you would do. So let's be honest, it is possible that you may have put yourself in that situation because had you listened to him, you wouldn't be in that predicament. I'm speaking from experience.

The other reason why God chooses not to answer or intervene at times hurts a whole lot more. I can't answer why God doesn't show up at times; only you and God know why you are going through what you are going through. There is a purpose for all things we go through, even the most hurtful things. That pain has a purpose. What you are going through is pushing you through to something greater. Here is my perspective on things because I have gone through some trauma that I can't necessarily explain. To help others out of darkness and pain, you oftentimes must meet them where they are – in that pain, in that darkness, in their trial, in that valley of shadows. The difference between you and them is you know the way out. So it is simple: you have to go through it to help them get through it. Think about it, somebody has helped you at different times in your life whether you realize it or not, now it is time for you to help them.

You will find purpose in your pain, triumph in your trial, victory in your valley, and determination in your darkness. You, my friend, are "built different." You are stronger than you think so remember who you are and whose you are. You are God's child; you are royalty. You don't belong in darkness; you are light. You are equipped with the tools to help others, so help your brothers and sisters out of their darkness because you know the way out. Just think about it – if your purpose wasn't so great, all that darkness wouldn't be thrown at you to try to keep you from fulfilling it. You must be destined for greatness; otherwise, your path would be easy.

Rise up and force the change by facing the challenge that lies ahead of you. You are an inspiration to so many others through the strength that you are displaying. Look how far you have come, so tell me, why you would stop now? They may try to keep you down, but clearly, they have yet to succeed – you are still standing, still breathing, still fighting, and you still have breath in your lungs. So get up and keep fighting; push through. You've got this! Besides, if you don't push through, who's going to go back and help others like you who are destined for greatness?

Remember, even in what we feel are our darkest moments, God's light, your light, will always shine through. You will realize that God's purpose for you is so great that you must keep him close to succeed. Obstacles and challenges will never stop coming, but the way you handle them will improve because you are now at the place where your ear is tuned into God's voice; and with him by your side, regardless of what happens, you will know it is okay because your Father is with you. He has never left you. He has always been there, and because of him, you are destined to succeed. **Stage 3** is when you relinquish all fear of your past and doubt of your future successes; you realize and recognize the strength and power God has given you to push through. Remember, the healing journey continues. You are stronger and wiser now.

This Day is Tough!

I'm going to go back in time for a little bit. I'm writing this now because, during my healing journey, I thought I had dealt with this. This was my unfinished business. This is the pain that resurfaced even after the awakening. During this phase of my healing journey, I had to face some things that I buried deep within; read this when you experience those tough days. Writing about this phase in my life is hard. I felt pain – I hurt everywhere – confusion, guilt, betrayal, fear, disgust, and shame. I desired escape; I wanted to run. My senses were heightened; I was ready to fight. You see, he had raped me before, but this time it was different. This one broke me; a portion of me died that day, and that portion of me began to rot. There has always been an innocence that resided in me – a sweet little girl, eager and willing to love, friendly, almost an angelic spirit, remained with me. This little girl would remind me of all my hopes and dreams. The girl in me had hope, inspiration, and an excitement for life. I loved her, but that day, I buried her; I let her go. The innocence in me was snatched out of me that day. The little girl who believed in love – the trusting one, the good one, the nice one – I buried her deep within my inner self, and I locked her in the room. I sent her away. I tucked my little girl and her innocence away inside a very dark room, in the corner, on a cold, wet floor, where she remained for quite some time. She was scared, uncertain, and confused as to why she was locked away.

After I locked her away, I boarded up the room and built a steel door that contained another vault with a code; only I knew the location of the vault and the code to enter. I took the code and hid it deep down in my heart; that was my way of protecting the core, the essence of me. And then, once I locked her away, reality set in, and I was back in the room with him. I fought.

I fought to get up and out of that room, to get away from him, to get from up under him, but he was too strong. I couldn't overpower him. I fought to get to a shower and wash all of that dirtiness and disgust off of me. I scrubbed vigorously, but I still couldn't come clean. I still felt dirty; I was so dirty that it made my stomach hurt. I felt like regardless of how much I scrubbed, I would just be drenched with the filth of his scent, sweat dripping on me, and his overpowering strength holding me down. I felt this repeatedly, but at least I looked clean on the outside. On the inside, my inner child was screaming for help. The adult in me said, "Quiet down now, little one, you can't come out, you can't survive in this world, and people will take advantage of you and hurt you, so I must keep you locked away," and went on with that day and pretended that everything was fine.

The LAST Violation

He had raped me before, but this time was the last time he was going to violate me. This was either the third or fourth time – sad that I lost count. The truth is I tried to block it out and pretend that it never happened each time it did. I just know that this time, something broke in me. I'm not talking about the little girl that I tucked away and hid; I'm talking about the original crack in my foundation, in my mind, in my spirit, in my soul – I broke. I can recall begging God that night; I begged and pleaded with God to make him stop. I begged him to please stop.

I kept telling him, "You are hurting me, you're hurting me." Then I would tell God, "He's hurting me, God, he's hurting me. Please make him stop, please God. It hurts; please make him stop." He hurt me so bad that night that my body stung from the pain he caused. I was so angry and so hurt that I embraced hate that night. At that moment,

I hated God because he didn't save me; because he could have. At least, that is what I told myself; he didn't protect me.

That night was so horrific for me because after I begged and pleaded for him to stop, I began to scream for help. There were other people in the apartment, but no one came to help me, no one. So, he had his way with me, he dirtied me, and he disgusted me. I went numb because once I prayed for help, screamed for help, and pleaded with him to stop and realized I couldn't fight my way out, I gave up, and I buried my face and screamed and just took it. I took all the pain, the dirtiness, the ugliness, and I tuned it out, but not before making a promise to myself that this would never happen to me again. I realized hate and anger were both strong, powerful emotions, so I clung to them, and that is how I survived with hate in my heart. I didn't hate God; I figured that there had to be a reason that he didn't come to my defense.

I was angry with God, but I hated myself. The girl in me that allowed this to happen, I hated her; I despised her. She was weak, vulnerable, gullible, pathetic, pitiful, an embarrassment. The brave girl in me was strong. The new version of me, she didn't have time for laughter or trust. She was always on guard; her defense mechanisms were always up, and my senses remained heightened. I was so alert and aware of my surroundings after that assault that

I could hear and see an ant crawling on the floor across the room on the carpet. Being on guard and alert all the time is not good; your body and your brain never rest. I had nightmares and panic attacks all the time. You get tired of living like that, pretending that you are fine, knowing deep down you are terrified. I needed to transition; it was time.

Now Is the Time

The pain, the hurt, the guilt, the frustration, the anger, the confusion, and the agony you feel when you make the decision to heal – it's all real. Know that once you decide to start your healing journey, you are on your way to finding your true purpose. You see, once you make a pact with God and you make your request known that you are ready and willing to heal, he responds in a way that is almost serene; something comes over you and within you. He takes your hand, and he leads you through your journey. Once you vocally and spiritually acknowledge that you are ready to heal, you won't be able to turn around because God won't let you. He wants the best for you and does not approve of the place you are in. You must realize that as your Father, who loves you dearly, he will always be there and help you out. Understand he won't do the healing *for* you, but he will walk alongside you and take the journey with you.

How does it begin, you ask? The first time I seriously questioned God and became angry with him was after the last time I was raped. You see, he had beaten me before. I didn't know or understand why this man felt he had to put his hands on me in that way, but I did heal; I always healed. The other times he raped me, it hurt, but I was able to hide it, bury my pain, and put it in that closet in that room behind that locked door. The time I cried out to God after I begged and pleaded with God to help me, and I felt as if he walked away from me, I began to question God.

I asked God, "Why did you let this happen to me? I thought you were supposed to protect me, help me. I mean, what did I do to deserve this? Why did you leave me, and why didn't you help?"

I remained in a dark place for a while. My pain turned into anger, my anger turned into fear, my fear turned into doubt, and my doubt turned into shame, embarrassment, guilt, and a feeling of unworthiness. All these emotions were so heavy and so dark that they began to consume me, but there is always a "but" with me. I remembered that I had light in me. I always had hope, I desired peace, and I had a burning desire in me to push through. Something in me constantly kept saying to me, *This can't be life. There has got to be more*. And there is always more.

I reminded myself that God, my God, my Father doesn't

want me here. This is not where I'm supposed to be. There is something more for me, so I took all that energy and harnessed it and placed it in one area, my job. My professional life took off. I focused all my energy on work and my son to create a better life for both of us. Without knowing, I was slowly beginning to heal; my attitude began to change, and I became more positive. Working with good people who work hard has a positive impact on you. Treating others with dignity and respect – and being treated with dignity and respect – caused me to slowly begin to look inward and love myself.

Personally, I dated, but I was fearful of men and very cautious of them. Because they were bigger than me, I felt they could easily hurt and kill me, rape me, or beat me. And if they decided to turn on me, mislead me, or hurt me emotionally, I knew I would blame myself because I wasn't sure if I was picking the right one. So, I kept my distance from men and only dated sporadically. Part of that distance was because I didn't trust my own judgment. I had been fooled and misled a few times, so I was always suspicious of a man's true intent. Living like this was draining. I was tired all the time from always being on the defense – until I got tired of being tired. I was tired of dealing with the uncertainty of relationships and my inability to know if I was making the right decision with those that I chose to date.

Overcoming my brokenness began years ago, but it was rocky. At times, I was right on track, and at other times, I pushed pause on my healing journey. I distanced myself from God when the pain from healing got too harsh or too much for me to bear. And that's when he separated and isolated me, and at that point, I couldn't run anymore.

I never had a problem being alone. I liked myself and valued alone time, but being isolated is a little different – I was forced to deal with my inner demons of pain, guilt, fear, embarrassment, and doubt. I was no longer angry; I realized I was just sad. I knew I deserved more; I just didn't know how to find my happiness. You see, God was working with and on me for years to get me where I needed to be, but I was always jumping ship when the pain got too real and too serious. He knew for me to truly heal emotionally and spiritually, I had to be in a place with little to no distractions. He also knew that once he helped me heal through the superficial layers, I would need his help to help me heal the deep-seated pain. It was now time to go deep and bring all that stuff up that I tried to bury, for me to understand my purpose and maintain my peace.

Self-awareness is a gift, meditation with God is a blessing, and self-love is priceless. When God sat me down and isolated me, at first, I was energetic and content to heal and get rid of all that pain and trauma. But when the actual healing process started, I said, *Oh God, wait, I don't think I am ready.* My healing prior to this was uncomfortable, but this healing was painful. I felt like he smiled and said, *I know, but that is why I am here.* And that's when the tears began to fall, and the pain began to resurface, and the anger reappeared, and the hurt – ohhhh the hurt, the fear, the uncertainty, the doubt, the sadness, the loneliness – all at once it seemed to resurface, and at moments, I didn't think it would ever end. I would find myself going to God and saying, *I think this is too much for me.* Notice, I never asked God to stop the healing process, nor did ever I ask him to take it away; I just pleaded with him and tried to explain that this is a little too overwhelming for me.

So, I started asking God to allow me to heal at a pace that I could manage, and almost immediately, I could breathe again and smile through the journey. God gave me relief; he helped carry my burden, but not until I asked him to. Some days were tougher than others, but he allowed me to breathe, rest, and smile through it all. What is crazy is I would say, *Okay God, I'm good now. I'm ready for what you have in store for me*, and then boom, again, I was hit with a ton of bricks. It was so heavy that, at times, all I could do was sit there and cry. Most of the time, I would be on my knees, and as I would be praying or just talking to God, the tears would just begin to fall as if my soul was cleansing itself. I couldn't stop the tears; I wasn't able to speak. I just felt emotions, but with the words I could utter, I said, *God, I need your help. Help me, please.* And my pain would slowly vanish, and the heaviness would leave.

Now understand, it took some time for me to call out to God to help take some of my burden away. I had to bear some of it myself to know how much pain, hurt, guilt, envy, and fear I was holding on to and carrying around with me every day. He needed to allow me to see how much weight and baggage I was choosing to hold on to. Sometimes, I would scream to try to release all that negative toxic energy; while other times, I would just take it, as the tears would silently roll down my face. What I do know is that God was with me the entire time. He never left my side, and those times I was laying on the bed or sitting against the wall alone in the dark, he was holding me. He was always holding me, and I thank him because even as I write this and the tears are falling, I have no pain, I'm no longer afraid, I'm no longer confused, there is no doubt, I have peace, I'm okay, I'm better, I'm stronger, I'm happy.

The tears that fall are tears of thankfulness, tears from the closeness I feel to God, and tears of happiness because for me to write this book, this chapter was a huge challenge. I had to believe in myself as I asked God to guide me through this one. What I do know is that it is only because of God that I am able to put my pain on paper in full display. You see, I don't have to hide my pain anymore, nor do I have to pretend that it did not exist. I am healed and still healing from my traumatic past. I can display my pain because it no longer consumes me, nor does it have a hold on me. What a blessing to know and understand the power we have with God on our side. The peace, the tranquility, and the happiness are so addictive and rewarding that I know I will not allow anyone or anything to ever compromise this feeling again. I pray, meditate, and talk to God every day and many times throughout the day. He is always with me, and I thank him for always being there. My prayer is that you allow him in so he can be there for you, too.

What If the Pain Comes Back?

It will come back; healing is a process, and it comes in phases. Just when you think you have dealt with something, some residual pain may come back just to make sure you are healed. This is what I'll tell you: It's okay to feel and acknowledge the pain. When you make the decision to go through the healing and cleansing process, you are telling yourself – your mind, body, and soul – that you are ready for the shift. You are inspired, excited, and determined at first to go through this process until you feel the weight of the pain, the heaviness of the guilt, the emptiness that is coupled with embarrassment, and the anger from the fear and the pain you once had. You will experience all of this before you experience a shift. Healing is a grieving process, and the pain often hits you when you least expect it. Here's how I recommend you deal with it when it comes back:

1. Acknowledge that this is what you asked and prayed for.
2. Ask God and your guardian angel (or angels) to help you through this. Note: We all have a guardian angel. At times when you are struggling with something specific, God often sends additional help. They are always there; however, they will only intervene when you ask them to.
3. Don't run from your feelings or emotions; feel it, cry, scream, sit, and breathe through it for however long you need to.
4. When it feels overwhelming, remember God is always with you to help you carry the weight; he never leaves you. When you feel as if you truly can't take it anymore, ask him to carry the weight and help lessen the burden so you can get through this. Remember, God is always listening, even if

you are just sitting in silence. Wait and feel the lift. Sometimes it is sudden when you feel the weight lifted, and other times it will happen gradually, often without you realizing. He will take up your cross, your burden, your pain, your grief, your fear, your anger, your doubt, your embarrassment, and he will give you peace.

When you are serious about your relationship with God, your growth and healing process will increase dramatically. When you prioritize God and make room for him, meaning when you create a time and make space for him daily to talk to and grow in him, your life will change. When you invite God into your life and your daily situation, your relationship will grow. Your safe place is for you and God; you clear your head, you remove all distractions, and you deliberately devote time for you and him. During this time, you will find that he speaks to you, answers your questions, and settles your spirit when needed. The result of you building a relationship with God will only increase your peace. When you speak with him daily, he will be accustomed to you coming to him, so when you go to him in times of emergencies, and in times of need, he is fully aware of who you are because of the relationship you chose to build with him and because of that relationship, he will bless you accordingly.

TAKEAWAYS FROM THIS SECTION

1. Acknowledge this is what you prayed for
2. Ask for Help from your guardian angels
3. Face your feelings don't run from them
4. Ask God to lessen the burden and feel the lift

> "To be who you are, after all you have been through at the hands of this world is beautiful."

PART

03

RECOGNIZING THE TRANSFORMATION

How to Move Forward in Love

Before we move on to the final portion of this book, I want to share something with you. The phrase "None of this is by Accident" came to me years before I wrote this book. I'm not sure when or why I chose to write it down, but I knew it would be the title of my book and that I would come back to it. I have read this book many times, and each time tears fall, because I see my growth and strength from this journey from the young confused girl to the wise mature woman I see in the mirror today. I don't know your challenges my friend, nor do I know your story. I'm not sure why certain things happened to you, nor do I understand it, but I do acknowledge and agree that it is not fair. No, I cannot explain why or what caused this and yes I know it hurts. This is what I can promise you, your life, your journey, your pain does not go unnoticed; it has a purpose.

What happened to you does not mean you are less than anyone or that you do not deserve the best in life unless you really choose to believe that about yourself (please don't, regardless of what anyone has said to you, it is not true). I stand by the statement "None of this is by Accident". This is your choice to use your pain to propel you into your purpose, pull from it, take control of your destiny and GO BE GREAT! Your journey is just as important as anybody else's; your story is being documented. Think about it: we are born with a purpose to fulfill, a purpose given to us by God. Along the way things occur to us to try to discourage and deter us from accomplishing our goal and fulfilling the purpose God sent you here to accomplish, especially if it is GREAT, which yours is.

You see sometimes, a lot of times, most of the time we forget why we were sent here. Have you ever noticed how kids are way more attuned to what is right without much guidance and how easily they are willing to help and share with each other? Somewhere they (we) get tainted, we grow distant from our innocence, and we become hardened exteriors of our former selves. I believe, prior to coming to earth we agreed to come here for a reason; our souls were sent here to accomplish something. Along the way we often forget our purpose because of all the trials and tribulations we face. It is up to us to dig deep and remember why we are here; we must tap into that childlike energy and ask God for his guidance to help us remember and fulfill his purpose. If you do not do this, we will have to answer for our actions or our inability to act. Imagine when our time does come to leave this Earth, and we arrive at our destination (whatever place you choose to believe), you get there and you remember everything you agreed to accomplish on Earth. But as your life is being shown to you, you see where you took the wrong turn, you see where you lost faith, you witness the moment where you could have overcome adversity, but you didn't. You gave up too soon, and you did not fulfill your purpose. The very thing you said you would come here to accomplish, you didn't. Now what?

Or, let's try a different version of this story: you get to your destination and your life journey is on display; but this time, you can see where you did pick yourself up again and kept going, where you found the courage, the strength, and the will to push through. You see where you pushed through all the uncertainty, all of the pain, guilt, fear, and shame. Imagine the smile on your face when you look back at your life and see how you overcame all that adversity. Imagine God looking at you saying, "Job well done, my good and faithful servant!" This is what I want you to focus on when you get discouraged, when you want to quit, when you feel like giving up. God put something in you that says get up, keep going, none of this is by accident! This is all a test!

This journey is hard; life is hard. I want you to make the best of it. So, sit down, reset, refocus, and realize that you have a mission that only you can accomplish. Now, regroup, strap on your boots, and let's get to it, my friend. Time is ticking and you have things to do. God put you here for a reason! What are you going to do about it – breakdown, crumble, and cry? Or get up, dust yourself off, put on your armor, hold your head up, stick your chest out, and walk out leading the pack of wolves that diligently and relentlessly tried to take you down? Get up, my friend, your journey is not over. It is supposed to be hard; this is what you signed up for. It will be challenging, and it won't be fair; but I promise you in the end, it will all be worth it! Like I said, none of this is by accident, including you reading this book. This is your reminder that you have a purpose. Your life is important, and your journey is required to accomplish your task. Allow this to put a fire up under you so that you can shake off all of the distractions, get it together, and finish what you came here to do. Now, let's close this thing out so you can get on with your life!

Learning to Wait Gracefully

We can often get frustrated and become rather impatient with God when we think we are ready for the next phase in our lives. We have the audacity to place demands on him or attempt to negotiate with God based on our selfishness at times. He loves us so much. I'm sure, like any good parent, he often chuckles and shakes his head at us. Sometimes, he chastises us; while other times, he allows us to go on a journey we chose for ourselves, knowing good and well it was not the route he directed, so he lets us see for ourselves. We must understand that our strength, our faith, and our growth occur in the waiting phase. If he gives us what we want and desire immediately or before we are ready to receive it, we don't always handle it the right way. We will not be appreciative of the blessing, nor will we be equipped or prepared to handle the blessing. He must build us up to ensure we have full trust, faith, and confidence that when we get what we asked for, we know beyond a shadow of a doubt that it is from him and only him, not our own doing. When we know it is from God, we handle our gift with care and are very cautious not to ruin it because we remember what it took to get it.

When our blessing is massive, he must ensure that we are properly and appropriately equipped to handle the magnitude of the blessing along with all the temptations or other distractions that may come with it. Trust in the Lord with all your heart and lean not to your own understanding. Acknowledge him in all thine ways, and he shall direct your path. Your healing will take place when you are no longer focused on the pain and the emotions but focused on the journey of reinventing your true self. Before you know it, you will find that you are smiling more, you are at peace, you understand the word and meaning of setting boundaries, and you know how to properly implement them. You begin to like yourself, which will transition into loving yourself. You will see and recognize your true strength, your power, and your own internal light. You will shine and sparkle without even trying. You will understand what true purpose and acceptance are and begin a new journey on your path to embrace your true purpose.

Your spirit will be at rest, not in turmoil, and your sense of peace will give you a calming, tranquil sensation. When you get off balance, and you are not feeling like yourself, you will have a path that lights up that will direct you back to your internal balance. Remember that throughout your healing phase, you must always continue to invite God into your life, to talk to him. We always need him; and we don't graduate from healing, we just transition to the next level or phase of healing. You will have setbacks, challenging days, and heavy emotions to deal with, but when you have those tough days, remember the steps, **acknowledge** – this is what you asked for; **ask for help** - spiritual guides are always willing to help; **feel it** - face it head on; you must go through it; you will come out on the other end stronger, wiser, and better; and **know God will be holding your hand** - he will be carrying you through the valley. Just know that you will come out on the other side of your healing journey stronger, better, and wiser.

Letting It All Go

When you have been taught to be strong or have had to be strong due to the nature of your circumstances your entire life, you begin to program your mind and body to always be strong, no matter what. This mindset is good when you must go through a tough time or a challenging journey, but there should come a time when you let go and allow yourself to breathe and relax. Relax and allow happiness and peace to come into your life. If you never give your body, mind, and soul the opportunity to relax, you will always operate in stress mode. You will wear yourself out and cause more strain and stress on yourself. When you are on guard constantly and you are constantly stressed, you will break mentally and sometimes physically, i.e. with injury or illness.

Think about the constant stress on a rubber band when you place too much tension on it; it breaks. Think about a blister that swells up with fluid; remember how tight the skin feels. Imagine a balloon when you put too much air in it; it pops. We don't realize this, but when we don't allow our bodies, our minds, or our spirit to relax to maintain its natural balanced state of homeostasis, we pop, we break, or we stretch ourselves so thin that the smallest agitation or friction will cause more pain to the touch like grazing a blister filled with fluid. Just the slightest touch or graze of the skin will cause unbearable pain. This is a physical representation of what we do to ourselves when we don't allow ourselves to have a break. This is how people blow up over the smallest things; because they have been holding on to so much stress for such a long time, they pop. We all must figure out how to allow time to unwind, relax, smile, and laugh. Be mindful and be in the moment, cherish your downtime, spend time with your loved ones, and smile anytime you can. Life is too short to live in a constant state of stress, and it doesn't help.

When you start to feel too overwhelmed, remember to breathe and to take it one day at a time, one step at a time; and before you know it, you will be working your way through your journey. When time permits you to relax, don't force yourself to get up. Take the time to relax and find your outlet to release some of that unwanted stress. You can pray, meditate, workout, read, sing, dance, create, take a walk in the park, play with the kids, watch TV, walk the dog, or just find a quiet place and just be. Whatever brings you joy and pleasure, do those things more frequently – as long as it is a healthy outlet. If drinking wine or alcohol is your stress relief, I wouldn't recommend drinking a whole bottle of wine to relieve your stress, but a glass every now and then is reasonable.

Find someone you can confide in, someone who will listen to you, someone who cares about you, or someone you can relate to – a therapist, a friend, a chaplain/minister/priest/pastor. Find someone you feel comfortable enough to open up to, to be honest and vulnerable with. We all need people in our lives that we can talk to. If you don't have anyone, I would say that this could be a sign that you are deliberately blocking people out of your life. If someone displays untrustworthy behavior, I understand not opening up to them. However, if you befriend someone and their patterns display that they are reliable and trustworthy, give them a shot; build a friendship and allow someone in your life to share your concerns with. A good, valuable, trustworthy friend is priceless. If you have healed, are going through the healing process, or have been holding on to any pain, hurt, betrayal, anger, or negative emotion, I'm telling you it's time to let go. Cry if you need to, scream, yell, sit in silence, breathe, feel it, acknowledge the feeling; Just don't allow your negative feelings or emotions to take up residence in your brain; allow hope and love in, even if it's a platonic friendship.

Discovering Love Again

Being vulnerable is a challenge after heartache and pain. Allowing someone close to your heart means you must expose your weaker and softer side to them. Our brain is wired to protect us from hurt and pain, including emotional pain. If we never heal from our emotional pain, we can often relive our emotional pain repeatedly. The problem is our brain does not realize that it is not really happening in the physical sense, so it is constantly being wired repeatedly to react to trauma and pain. For anyone to heal from trauma, it will require us to go through that pain again and revisit our past to rewire our brains from repeating that trauma. Know that most people shy away from that because it makes them feel weak and vulnerable again. But we must remember that we are stronger now, more mature, and wiser than before, which means we are able to revisit and deal with that pain as our older, wiser selves, knowing that we are strong enough to endure the healing process and come out on the other end better equipped and healed in order to let love in again. It is okay to let someone in after you have healed – and sometimes even during the healing process – if you are honest and transparent with that person about your healing journey.

You will know that you have matured and grown when you allow yourself to feel again, love again, smile again, and be happy. Your person should bring you peace. You should feel safe in their presence, like you don't have to pretend and that you can be your true authentic self. Learning to love yourself after trauma must occur before you can truly love someone else unconditionally. This is a challenge and not an easy journey because we are often our own worst enemy. Take it slow and remain consistent with your goal: to find and embrace your true, authentic, genuine self.

L – O – V – E: Let's Talk About It

Real love comes out of nowhere. The sensors in your brain begin to fire at an extremely rapid pace, and you find yourself smiling and glowing in a way that makes your entire body tingle. When God sends you love, the feeling consumes you; it's as if it blinds you because you cannot see, hear, think, or understand anything except the essence of that person. Their smile, voice, and touch cause you to stop and respond only to him or her – you are trapped in his/her aura. You are simply so captivated by their presence that you start to wonder how they got here. He/she just appeared not out of thin air.

But I wasn't looking for him/her – or maybe you were.

I was happy alone – but I am happier with him/her.

Content, at peace with myself, and I was open to love, praying for him/her and true unconditional love, but I wasn't searching. I was growing, healing, living, breathing, feeling, smiling, and loving me, and just like that he/she appeared.

You know you're healed when you can smile through it, your heart is consistent, your emotions are stable, and your conversation comes from a place of peace and tranquility, when the things that used to get you unsettled, frustrated, and irritated don't affect you anymore. When you can sit in silence without pain, grief, or guilt, when you don't spend your time apologizing because instead of saying the first thing that comes to your head, you sit and wait, and you only speak when it passes through three gates: Is it true? Is it necessary? Is it genuine? If what you have to say is not pleasing to God, sit with it, process it, hold it, and watch how it fades; he will take care of it for you. Just be patient and allow him to use you, work through you, and handle it better than you ever could.

Pray in silence when you are frustrated or if you are bothered unexpectedly by someone or something. He hears you; he's waiting for you to ask him for help. Remember, God goes before you, he walks with you, and he goes behind or after you when necessary. He's just waiting for you to realize and acknowledge that he has always been there, but more than that, he's waiting for you to trust him. When I find myself in these situations, I often begin talking to God. *I trust you, Lord. I trust your guidance;*

I trust your timing. I am your daughter, I am loved, I am safe, I am secure, I am protected. I am light. Your anointing flows through me and is renewing, restoring, and rebuilding every cell in my body back to perfect health, and I'm thankful for you. I am glad you created me; I am thankful for my journey, my path, my purpose, and my destiny. I can smile and laugh because of you; I am thankful and at a place of peace that only you could have provided. I am so happy and content to be loved by you, and I'm thankful that you are my father. I am beginning to see myself as you see me. My inner peace is so present and strong that I smile randomly because I feel your strength within me; I am so happy you are here.

By the time you finish thanking and acknowledging God, what bothered you before won't be so frustrating. Besides, don't ever allow someone to take you back to the person you were before your healing. Don't give anyone that much power over you. You have worked too hard to get this far. Ignore them and keep going. Pray for them, and when that doesn't work, pray for you.

Open Letter To My Husband

You are God-fearing. You have a relationship with God. You talk to God daily, you pray for me, and you must go through God to get to me. You are kind, attentive, gentle, passionate, masculine, caring, protective and handsome.

You love me in a way I've never been loved before, in a spiritual way, almost in a mystical way. You comfort me with your touch; you make me feel safe. You love me unconditionally. You caress me in a way that excites and calms me at the same time. God made you for me, and I'm so thankful for you. I've waited for you for quite some time now, and I'm so happy I did.

Thank you, God! I understand why I had to wait, and I'm so thankful that I did.

A Mother's Love

A mother's love is unexplainable. When you have a child, the love you have for them consumes you, and just like that, almost instantly, you would willingly give your last breath for the little miracle you and your partner created. You can sense their pain, and they can sense yours. Your survival skills increase significantly because your life is suddenly not as important as it used to be anymore, because their life is. Their safety, security, happiness, and desires are all that you care about – that's why the thought of losing a child or a child losing a mother is so debilitating. You can't rationalize how to live without them because they are all you know. Mothers love your sons and daughters, and children love your mothers; they are a blessing from God.

Only God can understand that type of love and the level of strength it takes to get over the loss of a mother or a loss of a child. He can help us with how to cope when we are forced to live without them. For those who have lost a child or a parent, may God hold your heart close, as he is the perfect one who can comfort you in those moments of despair. Allow him in; allow him to hold you, cover you, protect you, heal you, and comfort you in only the way he knows how. Rest on his shoulders. Understand that when the weight of despair, heartache, and pain, and grief gets too heavy or the burden gets too hard to bear, you can give it to him. He will take up your yoke and carry you the rest of the way. He is your father; he doesn't want any of his children to feel pain – he will fix it. His love is eternal and everlasting.

You will see them again. In the meantime, smell their scent, hug them tightly, and love them unconditionally; because when they are gone, and you begin to remember them, when the memories come back unexpectedly or when a scent reminds you of them, that is them letting you know that they are there with you, waiting, watching for the time and the moment where you will meet again.

To my readers, your healing journey is not like mine; it's like yours. Take your time, love yourself, find your peace, establish your boundaries, and create a balance that you are happy with. Your story and journey are just as important as mine. I hope this book helped you, and if it does, refer it to someone else and then go and help someone else through their journey. You would be surprised at how just one kind word can make someone's day. Be nice. Treat others with dignity and respect, and forgive others so you don't have to hold on to that hate and carry that unnecessary weight. Remember, the way people treat and act towards you has more to do with them than it does with you, so maybe, just maybe, they need to heal, too. Take care, and have a wonderful day. You are blessed, you are safe, you are worthy, and you are loved.

Takeaways from this section

1. Trust the process
2. Remember your journey and how far you come
3. No regrets just lessons learned

SOMETHING I WANT YOU TO REMEMBER

Once you start healing past traumas and your body comes out of flight or fight mode, your body will crave a lot of rest and silence. It will crave sunshine and water. Your body will finally start to feel safe in the peace, the quiet, the calm. Know this: you are not lazy; your body is just catching up on all the years it didn't have this stillness. Remember, my love, YOU DESERVE THIS!

ABOUT THE AUTHOR

Tanya R. Boudreaux, author of ***None of This is by Accident: My Testimony of Wholeness & Healing***, tells of an extraordinary journey into the life of a mother, soldier, and survivor. While reading, please envision and actualize the courage, determination and perseverance it took for Boudreaux to make it over the "rough side of the mountain".

She has taken dreadful, life-changing events and used them to fuel her fire, and believe me, that fire rages with biblical portions of tenacity. As God guides her steps, her resolve is strengthened through trials and tribulations that would've broken many men and/or women. Readers, I am humbled to introduce you to the woman that will one day change the world: the author, Tanya R. Boudreaux.

Made in the USA
Columbia, SC
22 July 2025